All rights reserved. No part of this publication may be reproduced in whole or in part, or stored in a retrieval system, or transmitted in any form, or by any means, either electronic, photocopying, recording, or otherwise, without written permission of Canopy Books.

Designed by Deena Fleming
© 2019 by Canopy Books, LLC
13319 Poway Rd
Poway, CA

Made and Printed in USA

These pages are packed with food knock knock jokes, animal knock knocks, school knock knocks, and much more that are guaranteed to tickle your funny bone. Drop these gems and watch as your audience erupts into laughter...or groans. Get ready, because the giggles are about to start!

Food Funnies

Knock, knock!
Who's there?
Bacon.
Bacon who?
I'm bacon a cake for your birthday!

Knock, knock!
Who's there?
Figs.
Figs who?
Figs the doorbell–it's broken!

Knock, knock!
Who's there?
Lettuce.
Lettuce who?
Lettuce in–we're cold!

Knock, knock!
Who's there?
Omelette.
Omelette who?
Omelette smarter than I look!

Knock, knock!
Who's there?
Queso.
Queso who?
It's a queso mistaken identity!

Knock, knock!
Who's there?
Yolk.
Yolk who?
Wanna hear a funny yolk?

Knock, knock!
Who's there?
Water.
Water who?
Water way to open the door!

Knock, knock!
Who's there?
Donut.
Donut who?
Donut forget to close the door behind me!

Knock, knock!
Who's there?
Ice cream.
Ice cream who?
Ice cream if you don't let me in!

Knock, knock!
Who's there?
Carrot.
Carrot who?
You don't carrot all!

Knock, knock!
Who's there?
Butter.
Butter who?
It's butter if you don't know!

Knock, knock!
Who's there?
Eggs.
Eggs who?
I'm eggs-cited to see you!

Knock, knock!
Who's there?
Peas.
Peas who?
Peas let me in!

Knock, knock!
Who's there?
Bean.
Bean who?
It's bean a while since I saw you!

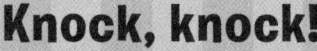

Knock, knock!
Who's there?
Taco.
Taco who?
Let's taco 'bout it!

Knock, knock!
Who's there?
Banana.
Banana who?

Knock, knock!
Who's there?
Banana.
Banana who??

Knock, knock!
Who's there?
Banana.
Banana who??

Knock, knock!
Who's there?
Orange.
Orange who? 
Orange you glad I didn't say banana?

Knock, knock!
Who's there?
Alva.
Alva who?
Alva 'nother piece of pie, please!

Knock, knock!
Who's there?
Barbie.
Barbie who?
Barbie-qued chicken is ready if you want some!

Knock, knock!
Who's there?
Broccoli?
Broccoli who?
Broccoli doesn't have a last name, silly!

Knock, knock!
Who's there?
Closure.
Closure who?
Closure mouth when you're eating!

Knock, knock!
Who's there?
Dee.
Dee who?
Dee-licious cookies for sale!

Knock, knock!
Who's there?
Geno.
Geno who?
Geno I don't like to eat broccoli!

Knock, knock!
Who's there?
Nacho.
Nacho who?
Nacho problem!

Knock, knock!
Who's there?
Grover.
Grover who?
Grover there and get me a cookie!

Knock, knock!
Who's there?
Hammond.
Hammond who?
Hammond eggs for breakfast please!

Knock, knock!
Who's there?
Oswald.
Oswald who?
Oswald my gum.

Knock, knock!
Who's there?
Ketchup.
Ketchup who?
Ketchup with me and I'll tell you!

Knock, knock!
Who's there?
Pasta.
Pasta who?
Pasta la vista, baby!

Knock, knock!
Who's there?
Pecan.
Pecan who?
Pecan somebody your own size!

Knock, knock!
Who's there?
Turnip.
Turnip who?
Turnip the volume—I can't hear the radio.

Knock, knock!
Who's there?
Xavier.
Xavier who?
Xavier fork for dessert.

Knock, knock!
Who's there?
Pizza.
Pizza who?
Pizza great guy, but he's away-that's why I came to your house!

What's in a Name?

Knock, knock!
Who's there?
Olive.
Olive who?
Olive you!

Knock, knock!
Who's there?
Dewey.
Dewey who?
Dewey have to go to school today?

Knock, knock!
Who's there?
Abe.
Abe who?
Abe B-C-D-E-F-G!

Knock, knock!
Who's there?
Adam.
Adam who?
Adam up and send me the bill!

Knock, knock!
Who's there?
Dwayne.
Dwayne who?
Dwayne the tub, I'm dwowning!

Knock, knock!
Who's there?
Justin.
Justin who?
Justin time for lunch!

Knock, knock!
Who's there?
Cameron.
Cameron who?
Cameron film are needed to take pictures!

Knock, knock!
Who's there?
Elly.
Elly who?
Elly-mentary, my dear Watson!

Knock, knock!
Who's there?
Ahmed.
Ahmed who?
Ahmed a mistake-can I borrow your eraser?

Knock, knock!
Who's there?
Maida.
Maida who?
Maida force be with you!

Knock, knock!
Who's there?
Howard.
Howard who?
Howard I know?

Knock, knock!
Who's there?
Doris.
Doris who?
Doris locked— that's why I'm knocking.

Knock, knock!
Who's there?
Luke.
Luke who?
Luke through the keyhole and you can see!

Knock, knock!
Who's there?
Wanda.
Wanda who?
Wanda door opens, I'll stop da knocking.

Knock, knock!
Who's there?
Ida.
Ida who?
Ida called first, but the phone's not working.

Funny Farm

Knock, knock!
Who's there?
Cows go.
Cows go who?
Cows go moo, not who!

Knock, knock!
Who's there?
Bach.
Bach who?
Bach, bach, I'm a chicken!

Knock, knock!
Who's there?
Goose.
Goose who?
Can you goose who it is?

Knock, knock!
Who's there?
Quack.
Quack who?
If you quack one more bad joke, I'm leaving!

Knock, knock!
Who's there?
Chicken.
Chicken who?
Just chicken up on you!

Knock, knock!
Who's there?
Quack.
Quack who?
Quack of dawn! Time to get up!

Knock, knock!
Who's there?
Goat.
Goat who?
Goat to the door and find out!

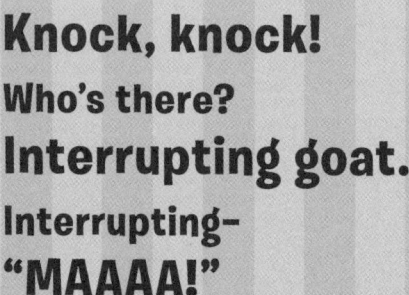

Knock, knock!
Who's there?
Interrupting goat.
Interrupting–
"MAAAA!"

Knock, knock!
Who's there?
Oink.
Oink who?
Make up your mind–are you a pig or an owl?

Knock, knock!
Who's there?
Herd.
Herd who?
Herd you were home!

Knock, knock!
Who's there?
Pig.
Pig who?
I'm here to pig you up!

Knock, knock!
Who's there?
Beef.
Beef who?
Let me in beef-fore I get angry!

Knock, knock!
Who's there?
Burro.
Burro who?
Can I burro some sugar?

Knock, knock!
Who's there?
Donkey.
Donkey who?
Unlock the door-this don-key doesn't work!

Funny Money!

Knock, knock!
Who's there?
Canoe.
Canoe who?
Canoe lend me some money?

Knock, knock!
Who's there?
Needle.
Needle who?
I really needle little money!

Knock, knock!
Who's there?
Robin.
Robin who?
Start robin the piggy bank— I need that money now!

Knock, knock!
Who's there?
Sparrow.
Sparrow who?
Can you sparrow dollar?

Knock, knock!
Who's there?
Cash.
Cash who?
I knew you were a nut!

Sports

Knock, knock!
Who's there?
Tennis.
Tennis who?
Tennis five plus five!

Knock, knock!
Who's there?
Adolf.
Adolf who?
Adolf ball hit me in da mouf, and now I talk dis way!

Knock, knock!
Who's there?
Europe.
Europe who?
Europe to bat!

Knock, knock!
Who's there?
Amy.
Amy who?
I'm always Amy for the top!

Knock, knock!
Who's there?
Dozen.
Dozen who?
Dozen anyone play soccer around here?

Knock, knock!
Who's there?
Meow.
Meow who?
Take meow to the ballgame!

Knock, knock!
Who's there?
Tahiti.
Tahiti who?
Tahiti home run you've got to swing hard!

Knock, knock!
Who's there?
Les.
Les who?
Les go and play hockey!

Knock, knock!
Who's there?
Uriah.
Uriah who?
Keep Uriah the ball!

Knock, knock!
Who's there?
James.
James who?
Oh, the James people play!

Knock, knock!
Who's there?
Scold.
Scold who?
Scold enough to go skiing!

Odds 'n' Ends

Knock, knock!
Who's there?
Broken pencil.
Broken pencil who?
Never mind—it's pointless!

Knock, knock!
Who's there?
Water.
Water who?
Water you doing in there?

Knock, knock!
Who's there?
Wendy.
Wendy who?
Wendy today, cloudy tomorrow!

Knock, knock!
Who's there?
Tree.
Tree who?
Have a tree-riffic day!

Knock, knock!
Who's there?
Wool.
Wool who?
Wool you please open the door?

Knock, knock!
Who's there?
Saturn.
Saturn who?
I Saturn my lunch!

Knock, knock!
Who's there?
Short-term memory loss.
Short-term memory loss who?
Knock, knock!

Knock, knock!
Who's there?
Jupiter.
Jupiter who?
Jupiter let me in now!

Will you remember me in an hour?
Yes.
Will you remember me in a day?
Yes.
Will you remember me in a week?
Yes.
Will you remember me in a month?
Yes.
Will you remember me in a year?
Yes.
I think you won't.
Yes I will.
Knock, knock!
Who's there?
See-you've forgotten me already!

Knock, knock!
Who's there?
Control freak.
Co...
You should say "Control freak who" now.

Knock, knock!
Who's there?
Don't be silly— opportunity doesn't knock twice!

Knock, knock!
Who's there?
Nobody.
Nobody who?
(Stay silent)

Gross-Out Knock-Knocks!

Knock, knock!
Who's there?
Seymour.
Seymour. who?
Seymour fleas in my hair?

Knock, knock!
Who's there?
Doug.
Doug who?
Doug a hole for the latrine yet?

Knock, knock!
Who's there?
Sue.
Sue who?
Sue me—I ate all the chocolate-covered ants!

Knock, knock!
Who's there?
Ty.
Ty who?
Ty a knot in that bag so the leeches don't crawl out.

Knock, knock!
Who's there?
Orange.
Orange who?
Orange you glad you don't have worms?

Knock, knock!
Who's there?
Canoe.
Canoe who?
Canoe please stop picking at your zits?

Knock, knock!
Who's there?
Betty.
Betty who?
Betty won't eat a slug!

Knock, knock!
Who's there?
Sara.
Sara who?
Sara booger hanging out of my nose?

Knock, knock!
Who's there?
Lettuce.
Lettuce who?
Lettuce use the bathroom or there's going to be an accident!

Knock, knock!
Who's there?
Will.
Will who?
Will you eat boogers for a dollar?

Knock, knock!
Who's there?
Ben.
Ben who?
Ben throwing up for days!

Knock, knock!
Who's there?
Keri.
Keri who?
Keri your own garbage bag!

Knock, knock!
Who's there?
Elise.
Elise who?
Elise you don't have boils.

Knock, knock!
Who's there?
Oswald.
Oswald who?
Oswald twelve worms and think I may throw up!

Knock, knock!
Who's there?
Kenny.
Kenny who?
Kenny really burp on command?

Knock, knock!
Who's there?
Urine.
Urine who?
Urine time for dinner!

Critters 'n' Creatures

Knock, knock!
Who's there?
Honeybee.
Honeybee who?
Honeybee nice and let me in!

Knock, knock!
Who's there?
Larva.
Larva who?
I larva you!

Knock, knock!
Who's there?
Roach.
Roach who?
Roach out next time you're in town!

Knock, knock!
Who's there?
Roach.
Roach who?
I roach you a letter—did you get it?

Knock, knock!
Who's there?
Abby.
Abby who?
A bee stung me on the nose!

Knock, knock!
Who's there?
Earl.
Earl who?
Earl-y bird gets the worm!

Knock, knock!
Who's there?
Omar.
Omar who?
Omar goodness, there's a ton of mosquitos

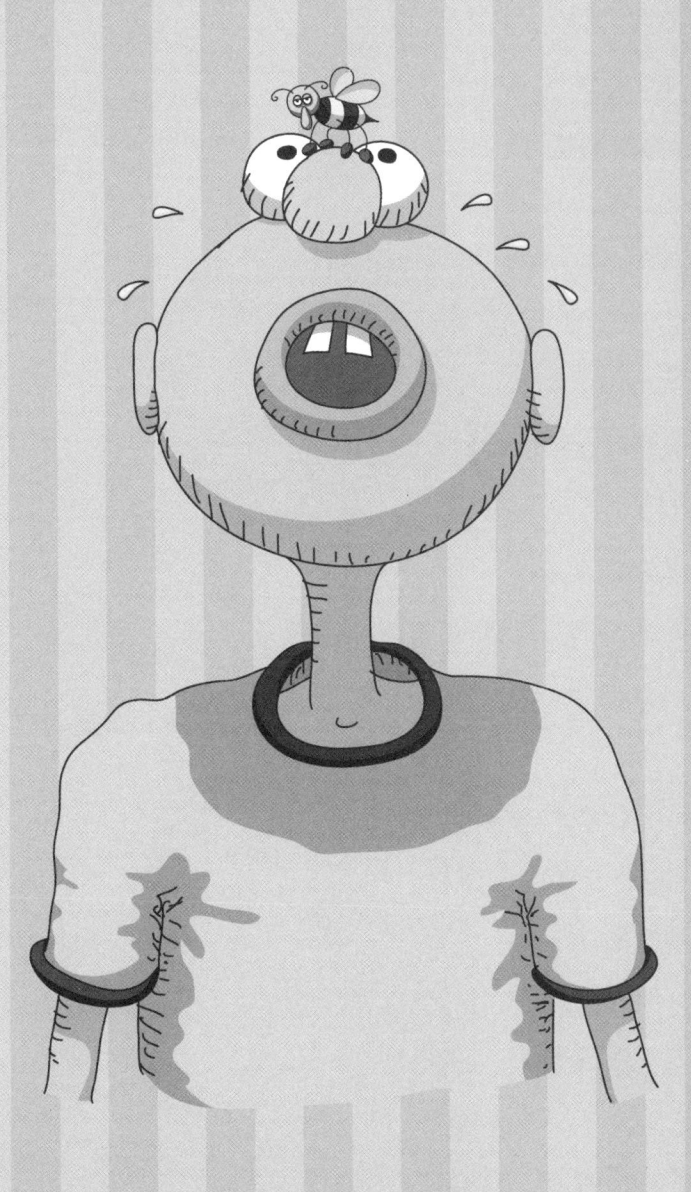

Knock, knock!
Who's there?
Achilles.
Achilles who?
Achilles mosquitos with a swatter!

Knock, knock!
Who's there?
Amos.
Amos who?
A mosquito bit me!

Knock, knock!
Who's there?
Ana.
Ana who?
Ana-ther mosquito!

Knock, knock!
Who's there?
Yetta.
Yetta who?
Yetta-nother mosquito!

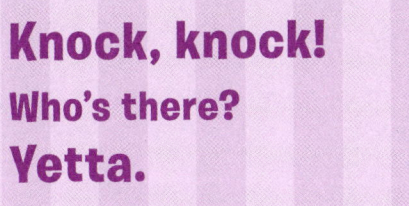

Knock, knock!
Who's there?
Beezer.
Beezer who?
Beezer in your hair!

Knock, knock!
Who's there?
Cass.
Cass who?
Cass more flies with honey than vinegar!

Knock, knock!
Who's there?
Spider.
Spider who?
Spider what everyone says, I still like you!

Knock, knock!
Who's there?
Thumpin.
Thumpin who?
Thumpin green and slimy is climbing up your back!

Knock-Knocks Gone Wild!

Knock, knock!
Who's there?
Cook.
Cook who?
Hey! Who are you calling cuckoo?

Knock, knock!
Who's there?
Raven.
Raven who?
What are you raven about?

Knock, knock!
Who's there?
Toucan.
Toucan who?
Toucan play this game!

Knock, knock!
Who's there?
Finch.
Finch who?
Finch me, am I dreaming?

Knock, knock!
Who's there?
Aardvark.
Aardvark who?
Aardvark a hundred miles for one of your smiles!

Knock, knock!
Who's there?
Alpaca.
Alpaca who?
Alpaca the suitcase; you load up the car!

Knock, knock!
Who's there?
Althea.
Althea who?
Althea later alligator!

Knock, knock!
Who's there?
Dinosaur.
Dinosaur who?
Dinosaurs don't go who—they go ROAR!

Knock, knock!
Who's there?
Janet.
Janet who?
Janet a big fish?

Knock, knock!
Who's there?
Moose.
Moose who?
Moose you be so nosy?

Knock, knock!
Who's there?
Some bunny.
Some bunny who?
Some bunny has been eating all my carrots!

Knock, knock!
Who's there?
Gorilla.
Gorilla who?
Gorilla me a steak.

Knock, knock!
Who's there?
Lion.
Lion who?
Lion on your front porch all day has been boring!

Knock, knock!
Who's there?
Panther.
Panther who?
Panther no panth, I'm going thwimming.

Knock, knock!
Who's there?
Impatient parrot.
Impatient par—
SQUAAWK!

Knock, knock!
Who's there?
Yvette.
Yvette who?
Yvette helps a lot of animals!

Spooky Laughs

Knock, knock!
Who's there?
Boo.
Boo who?
Don't cry—I'm not a ghost!

Knock, knock!
Who's there?
Ivana.
Ivana who?
Ivana suck your blood!

Knock, knock!
Who's there?
Wanda.
Wanda who?
Wanda ride on my broomstick?

Knock, knock!
Who's there?
Witch.
Witch who?
Witch one of you can fix my broomstick?

Knock, knock!
Who's there?
Witches.
Witches who?
Witches the way home?

Knock, knock!
Who's there?
Tyson.
Tyson who?
Tyson garlic around your neck to ward off vampires!

Knock, knock!
Who's there?
Fangs.
Fangs who?
Fangs for letting me in!

Knock, knock!
Who's there?
Harry.
Harry who?
Harry scary monster here to freak you out!

Cats 'n' Dogs

Knock, knock!
Who's there?
Aesop.
Aesop who?
Aesop I saw a puddy cat!

Knock, knock!
Who's there?
Cartoon.
Cartoon who?
Cartoon up just fine-she purrs like a cat!

Knock, knock!
Who's there?
Cat.
Cat who?
Cat you understand?

Knock, knock!
Who's there?
Catskills.
Catskills who?
Catskills mice!

Knock, knock!
Who's there?
Claws.
Claws who?
Claws the door—I'm getting cold!

Knock, knock!
Who's there?
Hans.
Hans who?
Hans off my kitten!

Knock, knock!
Who's there?
Hello.
Hello who?
Hello Kitty!

Knock, knock!
Who's there?
Purr.
Purr who?
Purr-fect kitty!

Knock, knock!
Who's there?
Puss.
Puss who?
Puss 'n' Boots!

Knock, knock!
Who's there?
Arthur.
Arthur who?
Arthur any more dogs out there?

Knock, knock!
Who's there?
Dash.
Dash who?
Dash-und!

Knock, knock!
Who's there?
Donut.
Donut who?
Donut pull my dog's tail, or he'll bite you!

Knock, knock!
Who's there?
Flea.
Flea who?
Flea from that dog before he bites us!

Knock, knock!
Who's there?
Ken.
Ken who?
Ken you walk the dog for me?

Knock, knock!
Who's there?
Patsy.
Patsy who?
Patsy dog on the head—he likes it!

Knock, knock!
Who's there?
Oliver.
Oliver who?
Oliver sudden my dog went crazy!

Knock, knock!
Who's there?
Pooch.
Pooch who?
Pooch your arms around me, baby!

Knock, knock!
Who's there?
Sarah.
Sarah who?
Sarah dog in there with you?

Knock, knock!
Who's there?
Senior.
Senior who?
Senior dog digging in the trash yesterday!

Knock, knock!
Who's there?
Theodore.
Theodore who?
Theodore is stuck, and my dog can't get out!

State Funnies

Knock, knock!
Who's there?
Alaska.
Alaska who?
Alaska my friend the question!

Knock, knock!
Who's there?
Arkansas.
Arkansas who?
I bet Arkansas wood faster than you can!

Knock, knock!
Who's there?
Ida.
Ida who?
It's not Ida who—it's Idaho!

Knock, knock!
Who's there?
Arizona.
Arizona who?
Arizona room for one of us in this town!

Knock, knock!
Who's there?
Hawaii.
Hawaii who?
I'm fine-Hawaii you?

Knock, knock!
Who's there?
Iowa.
Iowa who?
Iowa big apology to you!

Knock, knock!
Who's there?
Missouri.
Missouri who?
Missouri loves company!

Knock, knock!
Who's there?
Tennessee.
Tennessee who?
Tennessee you tonight?

Knock, knock!
Who's there?
Texas.
Texas who?
Texas are getting higher every year!

Knock, knock!
Who's there?
Utah.
Utah who?
Utah-king to me?

Get out of Town!

Knock, knock!
Who's there?
Cargo.
Cargo who?
Cargo better if you fill it with gas first!

Knock, knock!
Who's there?
Acid.
Acid who?
Acid down–you're rocking the boat!

Knock, knock!
Who's there?
Betsy.
Betsy who?
Betsy of all, it's a Cadillac!

Knock, knock!
Who's there?
Cargo.
Cargo who?
Cargo beep beep!

Knock, knock!
Who's there?
Carl.
Carl who?
Carl get you there faster than a bike!

Knock, knock!
Who's there?
Colin.
Colin who?
Colin all cars, Colin all cars!

Knock, knock!
Who's there?
Falafel.
Falafel who?
Falafel my bike and cut my knee!

Knock, knock!
Who's there?
Chooch.
Chooch who?
Are you pretending to be a train today?

Knock, knock!
Who's there?
Levin.
Levin who?
Levin on a jet plane!

Knock, knock!
Who's there?
Isabel.
Isabel who?
Isabel necessary for riding a bike?

Knock, knock!
Who's there?
Ivan.
Ivan who?
Ivan working on the railroad!

Knock, knock!
Who's there?
Mandy.
Mandy who?
Mandy lifeboats! The ship has hit an iceberg!

Knock, knock!
Who's there?
Mister.
Mister who?
Mister last bus home!

Knock, knock!
Who's there?
Philip!
Philip who?
Philip my gas tank, please—
I've got a long way to go!

Knock, knock!
Who's there?
Renato.
Renato who?
Renato gas for my car!

Knock, knock!
Who's there?
Dee Wilson.
Dee Wilson who?
Dee Wilson the bus go round and round.

Knock, knock!
Who's there?
Toyota.
Toyota who?
Toyota be a law against such awful jokes!

Knock, knock!
Who's there?
Wenceslas.
Wenceslas who?
Wenceslas train home?

Knock, knock!
Who's there?
Tank.
Tank who?
You're welcome!

Knock, knock!
Who's there?
Iona.
Iona who?
Iona new car!

Knock, knock!
Who's there?
Wanda.
Wanda who?
Wanda where I put my car keys!

School Funnies

Knock, knock!
Who's there?
Abe Lincoln.
Abe Lincoln who?
Aw, come on! Don't you know who Abe Lincoln is?

Knock, knock!
Who's there?
Aida.
Aida who?
Aida huge breakfast before school today!

Knock, knock!
Who's there?
Beto.
Beto who?
Beto school on time!

Knock, knock!
Who's there?
From.
From who?
Actually, it's from whom!

Knock, knock!
Who's there?
Rita.
Rita who?
Rita book-you might learn something!

Knock, knock!
Who's there?
Schnauzer.
Schnauzer who?
Schnauzer homework coming along?

Knock, knock!
Who's there?
Spell.
Spell who?
W-H-O!